The Hero

Essential Literary Themes

by Alexis Burling

Essential Library

An Imprint of Abdo Publishing | abdopublishing.com

abdopublishing.com

Published by Abdo Publishing, a division of ABDO, PO Box 398166, Minneapolis, Minnesota 55439. Copyright © 2016 by Abdo Consulting Group, Inc. International copyrights reserved in all countries. No part of this book may be reproduced in any form without written permission from the publisher. Essential Library™ is a trademark and logo of Abdo Publishing.

Printed in the United States of America, North Mankato, Minnesota
042015
092015

Cover Photo: Shutterstock Images
Interior Photos: Warner Brothers/Everett Collection, 13; Everett Collection, 15, 16, 23, 27, 33, 35, 36, 43, 46; Photofest Digital Library, 20; Universal Pictures/Newscom, 39, 40, 48; Jaap Buitendijk/TM/Fox Searchlight Pictures/Everett Collection, 55, 57, 59, 69; Francois Duhamel/TM/Fox Searchlight Pictures/Everett Collection, 61, 63, 71; Frederick M. Coffin and Nathaniel Orr, 65; Mary Evans Picture Library/Everett Collection, 77; Buena Vista/Everett Collection, 80; Mary Evans/Ronald Grant/Everett Collection, 83; Columbia/Everett Collection, 85, 89; Columbia Pictures/Everett Collection, 86; Columbia Pictures/Joseph Lederer/Newscom, 91; North Wind Picture Archives, 93

Editor: Jenna Gleisner
Series Designer: Maggie Villaume

Library of Congress Control Number: 2015931035
Cataloging-in-Publication Data

Burling, Alexis.
The hero / Alexis Burling.
    p. cm. -- (Essential literary themes)
Includes bibliographical references and index.
ISBN 978-1-62403-805-1
1. American literature--Themes, motives--Juvenile literature. 2. American literature--History and criticism--Juvenile literature. 3. Heroes in literature--Juvenile literature.   I. Title.
810--dc23
                                                                                                2015931035

Contents

1

Themes in Literature

D o you find yourself drawn to the same types of stories? Are your favorite characters on a quest? Are they seeking revenge? Or are your favorite stories about love? Love, revenge, a quest—these are all examples of themes. Although each story is different, many stories focus on similar themes. You can expand your understanding of the books you read by recognizing the common themes within them.

What Is a Theme?

A theme is a concept or idea that shows up again and again in various works of art, literature, music, theater, film, and other endeavors throughout history. Some themes revolve around a story's plot. For example, a play about a young girl moving away from home and learning the ways of the world would be considered a coming of age story. But themes are not always so easily noticed. For example, a work might have allusions. Allusions are references, sometimes indirect, to other works or historical events. Themes might also relate to specific characters or subjects of a work. For example, many stories present heroes or villains. These common character types are often called archetypes.

How Do You Uncover a Theme?

Themes are presented in different ways in different works, so you may not always be aware of them. Many works have multiple themes. Uncover themes by asking yourself questions about the work. What is the main point or lesson of the story? What is the main conflict? What do the characters want? Where does the story take place? In many cases, themes may not be apparent until after a close study, or analysis, of the text.

What Is an Analysis?

Writing an analysis allows you to explore the themes in a work. In an analysis, you can consider themes in multiple ways. You can describe what themes are present in a work. You can compare one work to another to see how the presentation of a theme differs between the two forms. You can see how the use of a particular theme either supports or rejects society's norms. Rather than attempt to discover the author's purpose in creating a work, an analysis reveals what *you* see in the work.

Raising your awareness of themes through analysis allows you to dive deeper into the work itself. You may begin to see similarities between all creative works that you encounter. You may also improve your own writing by expanding your understanding of how stories use themes to engage readers.

Forming a Thesis

Form your questions about how a theme is presented in a work or multiple works and find answers within the work itself. Then you can create a thesis. The thesis is the key point in your analysis. It is your argument about the work. For example, if you want to argue that the theme of a book is love, your thesis could be worded as follows: Allison Becket's novel *On the Heartless Road* asserts that receiving love is critical to the human experience.

How to Make a Thesis Statement

In an analysis, a thesis statement typically appears at the end of the introductory paragraph. It is usually only one sentence long and states the author's main idea.

Providing Evidence

Once you have formed a thesis, you must provide evidence to support it. Evidence will usually take the form of examples and quotations from the work itself, often including dialogue from a character. You may wish to address what others have written about the work. Quotes from these individuals may help support your claim. If you find any quotes or examples that contradict your thesis, you will need to create an argument against them. For instance: Many critics claim the theme of love is secondary to that of revenge, as the main character, Carly, sabotages the lives of her loved ones throughout the novel. However, the novel's resolution proves that Carly's experience with love is the key to her humanity.

Concluding the Essay

After you have written several arguments and included evidence to support them, finish the essay with

How to Support a Thesis Statement

An analysis should include several arguments that support the thesis's claim. An argument is one or two sentences long and is supported by evidence from the work being discussed. Organize the arguments into paragraphs. These paragraphs make up the body of the analysis.

a conclusion. The conclusion restates the ideas from the thesis and summarizes some of the main points from the essay. The conclusion's final thought often considers additional implications for the essay or gives the reader something to ponder further.

How to Conclude an Essay

Begin your conclusion with a recap of the thesis and a brief summary of the most important or strongest arguments. Leave readers with a final thought that puts the essay in a larger context or considers its wider implications.

In This Book

In this book, you will read summaries of works, each followed by an analysis. Critical thinking sections will give you a chance to consider other theses and questions about the work. Did you agree with the author's analysis? What other questions are raised by the thesis and its arguments? You can also see other directions the author could have pursued to analyze the work. Then, in the Analyze It section in the final pages of this book, you will have an opportunity to create your own analysis paper.

The Hero

The book you are reading focuses on the theme of heroes. Heroic characters in literature, art, and film are those who accomplish extraordinary deeds. They change the way we think about our lives and see the world. Some, such as Odysseus or Huckleberry Finn, are fictional characters who overcome obstacles in the face of adversity. Others, such as Gandhi or Martin Luther King Jr., are real-life saints in history. But what exactly is a hero? Are there common personality traits or flaws? Must heroes, by definition, embrace society's values and rules, or can they challenge established norms? Authors use heroic characters to provide examples of model behavior. In understanding the heroes' motivations and struggles, we can better understand how to live more courageous lives and inspire others to do the same.

Look for the Guides

Throughout the chapters that analyze the works, thesis statements have been highlighted. The box next to the thesis helps explain what questions are being raised about the work. Supporting arguments have also been highlighted. The boxes next to the arguments help explain how these points support the thesis. The conclusions are also accompanied by explanatory boxes. Look for these guides throughout each analysis.

2

AN OVERVIEW OF

Harry Potter and the Sorcerer's Stone

*H*arry Potter and the Sorcerer's Stone is the first of seven books in J. K. Rowling's internationally best-selling series about a young boy with magical powers. It was published on June 26, 1997, to worldwide critical acclaim and was adapted into a movie in 2001.[1] The film, directed by Christopher Columbus and starring Daniel Radcliffe (Harry Potter), Rupert Grint (Ron Weasley), and Emma Watson (Hermione Granger), chronicles Harry's beginnings as an orphan, as well as his eventful first year at Hogwarts School of Witchcraft and Wizardry.

Daniel Radcliffe plays the character of Harry Potter in all eight Harry Potter films.

Miserable at the Dursleys'

In the movie's opening scene, Albus Dumbledore, the wise headmaster of Hogwarts, and Professor McGonagall, the head of Gryffindor House, whisper to each other outside 4 Privet Drive in Surrey, England, about an orphaned infant named Harry Potter. Hagrid, the oafish groundskeeper of Hogwarts, descends from the sky on his flying motorcycle and hands the two wizards a baby wrapped in blankets.

"This boy will be famous," says Professor McGonagall as she gazes down at Harry and the lightning bolt scar on his forehead. "There won't be a child in our world who doesn't know his name."[2]

"He's far better off growing up away from all that . . . until he's ready," replies Dumbledore.[3]

McGonagall and Dumbledore deliver Harry to the doorstep of Harry's aunt and uncle, Petunia and Vernon. As Harry grows into a young boy over the next ten years, his childhood with the Dursleys is anything but idyllic. Uncle Vernon is a blundering fool, while Aunt Petunia spends her days doting on their spoiled son, Dudley. Harry sleeps in a cramped closet

Harry is at first surprised by his magical ability.

beneath the stairs and is either tormented by Dudley or
ignored altogether.

But soon strange events start occurring. One
day while at the zoo, Harry magically locks the
tantrum-pulling Dudley in a python's cage. Then
invitations to Hogwarts appear for Harry, first in the
mailbox, then dozens through the chimney. Soon there
are so many letters Vernon and Petunia are forced to
shuttle Harry and Dudley off to a remote island where
no one—and no mail—can reach them. No one, that
is, except Hagrid. On Harry's eleventh birthday, Hagrid
breaks down the door of the Dursleys' island shack,
tells Harry the truth about his wizardly heritage, and
whisks him off to London, England, to prepare to
attend Hogwarts.

Despite the thousands of letters that invade the Dursleys' home, Harry is not allowed to open them, even though they are all addressed to him.

The Journey to Hogwarts

From the moment Harry arrives in London, he is flabbergasted by what he sees—especially when Hagrid takes him to Diagon Alley, a hidden street where a dizzying array of magic-related supplies are on display. Owls sit in cages. Wands magically choose their wizards. The new Nimbus 2000—the fastest Quidditch broom on the market—appears in a store window. Harry buys everything he needs, and after a quick stop at Gringotts bank, where Hagrid retrieves a mysterious package from a vault, the two head to the train station.

On the way, Hagrid tells Harry about Voldemort, the wizard-gone-bad who has thousands of followers.

Voldemort killed Harry's parents because they refused to get out of his way. Other than a scar burned into his forehead, baby Harry survived the attack without harm. "Something about you stumped him that night," Hagrid tells Harry. "That's why you're famous. . . . You are the boy who lived."[4]

Before Harry can ask anything else, Hagrid disappears. Luckily, a cheerful woman named Mrs. Weasley helps Harry get to Platform 9 ¾, advising him to run full speed at a brick wall between platforms 9 and 10. When the Hogwarts Express chugs into the train station, Harry shares a cabin with Mrs. Weasley's youngest red-haired son, Ron. Later, the two meet precocious Hermione Granger.

Learning to Be Wizards

From the moment Harry, Ron, and Hermione arrive at Hogwarts, they are swept up in a flurry of activity. First they are sorted into residential houses by the magical sorting hat. All three and a few others are assigned to Gryffindor, while the rest of the first years are divided between the Hufflepuff, Ravenclaw, and Slytherin houses. Harry makes an immediate enemy of bully

Draco Malfoy, who is chosen for Slytherin, Voldemort's onetime house.

Then the students cycle through their courses. Learning to fly their brooms causes the most excitement, especially when Malfoy and Harry get into a heated one-on-one match on their brooms. Both boys are punished for flying without permission, but Harry is chosen to be Gryffindor's Quidditch seeker because of his speed and skill. Quidditch is a sport similar to soccer but played on brooms.

Harry, Ron, and Hermione encounter trouble when they discover a secret room on the forbidden third floor. After Hermione uses a spell to unlock the door, the three are shocked to find a giant three-headed dog sitting on a trapdoor. The three race back to their dormitory to avoid getting caught, but they make a pact to uncover what the beast is guarding.

More Trouble Afoot

Despite the trio's discovery, life at Hogwarts stays relatively calm until Halloween night, when the Defense Against the Dark Arts professor, Quirrell, storms into the dining hall, yelling that a troll is on the grounds. Everyone flees except Hermione, who had locked herself in the girls' bathroom earlier after Ron called her a brownnoser. Harry and Ron rush to her rescue only to find the troll in the same bathroom. The three defeat the troll using a combination of smarts and magic. When their teachers barge in and Hermione takes part of the blame, the friendship between Harry, Ron, and Hermione is cemented.

The troll incident is the least of Harry's problems. When he sees a gash on Potions Professor Snape's leg, he suspects Snape let in the troll as a distraction in order to steal what's beneath the trapdoor. Then later when Snape seemingly puts a curse on Harry's broom during a Quidditch match, Harry, Ron, and Hermione share their suspicions about Snape with Hagrid. Hagrid refutes their theory, telling them the three-headed dog is guarding a secret known only to Dumbledore and a man named Nicholas Flamel.

Harry uses an invisibility cloak he received as a Christmas present to access the restricted section of the library to research Flamel. He also discovers the Mirror of Erised in an old classroom. Dumbledore explains to Harry that the mirror reveals the deepest desires of whoever looks into it. Then Hermione finds a book revealing the identity of Flamel and shares it

Harry breaks the rules by sneaking into the restricted part of the library, wearing his invisibility cloak.

with Ron and Harry. According to the book, Flamel was an alchemist who created the Sorcerer's Stone—a stone that produces an elixir that grants its drinker immortality. This, they realize, is what the three-headed dog is guarding.

Voldemort Returns

Days later, Harry, Ron, Hermione, and Malfoy receive detention. As punishment, they are sent into the Forbidden Forest with Hagrid to search for an injured unicorn. Harry stumbles upon the dead beast and, beside it, a cloaked figure. The cloaked figure is Voldemort, and he's drinking the unicorn's blood to build up strength so he can obtain the Sorcerer's Stone.

Harry, Ron, and Hermione make a plan to retrieve the Sorcerer's Stone before Voldemort can. When they reach the trapdoor that night, someone has lulled the three-headed dog to sleep with harp music. They dive into the trapdoor, only to be entangled by a plant called the Devil's Snare. Hermione's knowledge of the plant helps them escape. Next they encounter a room full of flying keys. Harry uses his Quidditch skills to snag the correct key to unlock the door. Finally, Ron battles it out in a violent game of chess. He sacrifices himself so that Harry can check the king and go on alone.

What Harry encounters in the final room is a surprise: Professor Quirrell standing in front of the Mirror of Erised. Harry looks at his reflection and spots the Sorcerer's Stone in his pocket. When he lies to Quirrell about what he sees, Voldemort appears in the back of Quirrell's head and demands that Harry hand over the stone in exchange for the return of his parents. Harry refuses and uses a spell to turn Quirrell's body to stone. Voldemort vanishes into thin air.

Later, Dumbledore destroys the stone and Voldemort is foiled for the time being. Hermione, Ron, and Harry say their good-byes for the summer, already looking forward to their next year—and adventures— at Hogwarts.

Harry Potter as Anti-Archetype

*W*hen thinking about the archetype, or typical example, of a hero, what common qualities come to mind? Superhuman strength? Undeniable genius? But what about characters who may not be extraordinary in any way? Can't they also be considered heroes? When analyzing the role of heroes in film, it's important to recognize that it is often the more humble characters—those who acknowledge their own shortcomings and who aren't afraid to ask others for help—that stretch the boundaries of human potential and achieve remarkable feats despite seemingly insurmountable odds.

Harry arrives at Hogwarts with a distinct advantage over the other students—a glowing reputation for surviving Voldemort's attack on his parents, James

Harry plays the humble yet brave hero in *Harry Potter and the Sorcerer's Stone*.

Thesis Statement

At the end of the first paragraph, the author states the thesis: "But unlike archetypal heroes who might use wealth or status to their advantage, it's Harry's unassuming qualities—his innate humility, reliance on teamwork, and selfless desires—that enable him to obtain the Sorcerer's Stone and heroically defeat Voldemort." This essay will focus on the characteristics of Harry that make him a hero.

Argument One

Next, the author begins to support her thesis by presenting the first argument, using concrete examples of Harry's humble beginnings as an orphan: "A typical hero might fight back against those who wrong him, but Harry rises above hardship by acting humbly."

and Lily Potter. But unlike archetypal heroes who might use wealth or status to their advantage, it's Harry's unassuming qualities—his innate humility, reliance on teamwork, and selfless desires—that enable him to obtain the Sorcerer's Stone and heroically defeat Voldemort.

A typical hero might fight back against those who wrong him, but Harry rises above hardship by acting humbly. After Voldemort murders his parents and Harry is orphaned, Harry must spend his formative years under the care of the Dursleys. Despite the less-than-ideal arrangement, Harry doesn't start tantrums or make trouble. Instead, he mostly stays out of the Dursleys' way and acts the obedient son.

The Dursleys do everything in their power to make Harry's existence miserable. While their bratty son Dudley luxuriates in a spacious bedroom and receives numerous gifts on holidays, Harry sleeps in a tiny closet with hardly a book to his name. He also suffers through Dudley's runs up and down the stairs without complaint, bearing the dust that rains down on his bed and greeting each new affront with a smile. Even when dozens of Hogwarts invitations flood the Dursleys' home and their island hiding place, Harry never opens one without permission. It takes an intervention from Hagrid, who physically removes Harry from the island and tells him about his wizardly roots, for Harry to break free from the Dursleys' clutches.

Once he arrives at Hogwarts, Harry goes against what an archetypal hero often does by easily acknowledging his peers' strengths and relying

Argument Two

The author then presents the second argument. She begins by discussing why Harry's willingness to collaborate instead of depending on his own reputation helps him accomplish heroic deeds: "Once he arrives at Hogwarts, Harry goes against what an archetypal hero often does by easily acknowledging his peers' strengths and relying on teamwork to accomplish goals for the common good."

on teamwork to accomplish goals for the common good. Though naturally gifted in Quidditch like his father, Harry proves his talent for being a seeker. When he snags the Golden Snitch and wins the game during one of his first matches, he doesn't brag. A win for Gryffindor is more important. He shows the same willingness to collaborate when battling the club-wielding troll in the girls' bathroom. Instead of saving his own hide and leaving Hermione to her fate, Harry enlists Ron, who chants the Wingardium Leviosa spell that levitates the troll's club. Together they defeat the giant beast.

Harry's race to gain possession of the Sorcerer's Stone toward the end of the movie provides, perhaps, the clearest example of why teamwork and Harry's atypical heroism go hand-in-hand. Harry checks in with Hagrid and Dumbledore throughout his first year at Hogwarts to hear their knowledge and advice. But by acknowledging his limitations and relying on his peers—Hermione's smarts to get past the Devil's Snare and Ron's aptitude for chess to check the king during the final few scenes—Harry is able to advance past obstacles that would have hindered him if he had

Ron helps Harry defeat the troll and save Hermione.

undertaken the task of fighting Voldemort and retrieving the stone alone.

Finally, the selfless nature of Harry's desires is what makes him a true hero. When Harry gazes into the Mirror of Erised, he doesn't see himself as an all-powerful ruler of Hogwarts as an archetypal hero might. He also doesn't see himself pampered by success and riches, as someone like Malfoy would. Instead, Harry longs to be reunited with his loving parents and vows to avenge their wrongful deaths, no matter the risks.

Argument Three

The author finishes proving her thesis by providing a third argument. Here, she states the culminating reason why Harry can be considered the most heroic character in the movie: "Finally, the selfless nature of Harry's desires is what makes him a true hero."

So, too, when Harry realizes he's holding the Sorcerer's Stone in his pocket, he doesn't drink the elixir of life, nor does he accept Voldemort's promise to bring his parents back to life. Rather, Harry refuses to hand over the stone to Voldemort, who would use its powers for evil. "Only a person who wanted to find the stone—find it but not use it—would be able to get it,"[1] Dumbledore reveals to Harry after the ordeal is over.

Harry Potter isn't an archetypal hero—the epitome of brawn or might. Nor could he ever be considered a genius, especially with Hermione by his side. But the humble and openhearted orphan wants the best for his friends and even, some might argue, for his enemies. It is for this reason he is the film's most heroic character.

Conclusion

The final paragraph is the conclusion, in which the author summarizes the arguments made throughout the paper and restates the thesis using different language. In this essay, the conclusion reiterates the idea that, although Harry Potter isn't an archetypal hero, it's because of his humility, reliance on his friends' help, and selfless approach to life that he is nonetheless considered the film's most heroic character.

Thinking Critically

Now it's your turn to assess the essay. Consider these questions:

1. The author's thesis statement asserts that Harry's humility, acceptance of others' help, and unassuming goals enable him to defeat Voldemort at the end of the film and fulfill the role of hero. Do you think the arguments effectively support this thesis? Why or why not?

2. The author suggests Harry is a hero even though he doesn't fit the archetype. Do you agree? Is there evidence in the film that could disprove this theory?

3. What parts of the author's argument did you find most convincing? Is there any evidence you could add to this critique to strengthen the author's argument?

Other Approaches

The previous essay was only one way to analyze the theme of heroic archetype in *Harry Potter and the Sorcerer's Stone*. Another analysis might compare and contrast minor archetypal heroes in the film to see how they match up to Harry. Still another analysis might argue that, although Harry exhibits noble qualities, part of what makes him an anti-archetypal hero is his willingness to rebel to achieve his goals.

Anyone Can Be a Hero

Harry Potter is the most obvious heroic figure in the film. But there are other characters who display honorable qualities as well: Hermione for her smarts and Ron for his inherently good-natured attitude. Though books and films usually contain one primary heroic protagonist, it's often worth examining other characters' talents and motivations and how those qualities impact the course of the story. A thesis for an essay exploring these ideas might read: By creating other characters who possess a variety of heroic qualities in addition to Harry, J. K. Rowling teaches readers

that each and every character has the power to shine in some way.

Heroes as Rule-Breakers

At the end of the film, Harry saves the day. But that doesn't mean he's perfect. In fact, Harry rebels against authority quite a bit throughout his first year at Hogwarts. For example, he accesses the restricted section of the library and ventures into the forbidden third floor's trapdoor. Many critics might argue that it's Harry's willingness to flout authority that makes him an archetypal hero. A possible thesis statement arguing this idea might be: It is Harry's eagerness to think for himself and bend the rules for the right reasons that makes him a flawed but likable and heroic character.

AN OVERVIEW OF

To Kill a Mockingbird

The novel *To Kill a Mockingbird* by Nelle Harper Lee was published on July 11, 1960. Set in the sleepy fictional town of Maycomb, Alabama, in the early 1930s during the Great Depression, the story is told in two parts and narrated in the first person by six-year-old Scout Finch. Scout describes events both as they unfold over the course of three years and in retrospect, looking back on what transpired as an adult.

As Lee's novel opens, Scout paints a portrait of her hometown: "[It was] a tired old town . . . there was no hurry, for there was nowhere to go, nothing to buy and no money to buy it with, nothing to see outside the boundaries of Maycomb County."[1] Along with her

Mary Badham, *left*, and Phillip Alford, *right*, played Scout and Jem in the 1962 film *To Kill a Mockingbird*.

widowed father, Atticus, a lawyer and representative in the state legislature, and Calpurnia, the Finches' black cook and caretaker, Scout lives on Main Street with her brother, Jem, who is four years older and entering fifth grade.

Through the sticky days of June, July, and August, Scout and Jem spend their days goofing off in the backyard with Charles Baker Harris, or "Dill," the curiously dressed seven-year-old boy who arrives to spend the summer with his Aunt Rachel, the Finches' neighbor. The kids' favorite game is acting out imaginative skits involving the Radleys, the reclusive family who lives in the dilapidated house three doors down. They also think up ways to make the neighborhood legend Arthur Radley, known as "Boo," leave the house after his father locked him inside 15 years earlier as punishment for a teenage prank gone awry.

Trouble in First Grade

Scout is a tomboy with a feisty temper. On the first day of first grade, she gets in trouble for a slew of infractions—learning to read too early, for one (thanks

Jem, Scout, and Dill, *right*, are fascinated with Boo, the town's recluse, and often spy on his house.

to Atticus's help). She also sasses Miss Caroline, the new teacher, for not knowing the ways of Maycomb.

Later that evening when Scout returns home, she begs her father to let her stay home from school for the rest of the year. But Atticus will not give in. He advises Scout to think of things through other people's point of view to better understand them. He says that will be Scout's way of getting along better with the other kids at school.

The rest of the year passes without incident. On the last day of school, Scout and Jem uncover a mysterious present inside the knothole of one of the Radleys' oak

Jem and Scout discover small gifts in the knothole of the Radleys' oak tree.

trees: a tiny box covered in chewing gum wrappers containing two Indian-head pennies. Two days later, Dill arrives for another summer in a flurry of excitement, and the obsession of embellishing and acting out the Radleys' tragic story is renewed.

Their first attempt at making Boo come out by attaching a note to a fishing pole and slipping it through a broken window shingle is ruined. Atticus catches them in the act and gives them a lecture. Their second try doesn't go any better. When they sneak out to peek in the Radleys' back window, a shotgun blast sends them scurrying through the night and over a fence. They would have gotten away with it if Jem hadn't lost his pants on the barbed wire fence. When he finds them the next day—neatly folded right where he lost them—he feels ashamed, though curious about who might've been responsible for returning the pants.

Learning Hard Lessons

As autumn rolls into winter, Scout slogs through second grade. Boo's cranky older brother Nathan seals the knothole up with cement. And Miss Maudie's house next door catches on fire and is destroyed in the blaze. Then Scout and Jem notice an uptick in teasing at school. Their racist cousin Francis criticizes Atticus for agreeing to defend Tom Robinson, a black man accused of raping a white woman, in an upcoming court case. Even sickly old Mrs. Dubose joins in on the taunting when she spits out, "Your father's no better than the niggers and trash he works for."[2] Jem swipes the tops off of every camellia in Mrs. Dubose's yard in retaliation.

Despite the cruelty of the remarks, Atticus doesn't let Jem get away with his actions. Instead, he orders

Jem and Scout to read to Mrs. Dubose for a month. He also gives them a stern but compassionate talking-to: "It's not fair for you and Jem, I know that," he explains. "This case, Tom Robinson's case, is something that goes to the essence of a man's conscience. . . . I couldn't go to church and worship God if I didn't try to help that man. . . . Before I can live with other folks I've got to live with myself."[3]

Tom Robinson's Trial

The summer Jem turns 12 brings much excitement, both good and bad. Dill is back in town, though this time he ran away from his neglectful parents. Scout and Jem learn more about the black community by attending church services with Calpurnia. And Atticus's sister, snooty Aunt Alexandra, moves in and takes charge of the household while her brother spends more time at the office preparing Tom Robinson's defense.

The night before the court case begins, an angry mob, disgusted by Robinson's supposed crime, threatens to lynch him. But Atticus—with the help of Scout and Jem—stands guard outside the jail and diffuses the situation by speaking to the men as equals. On the day of the trial, as one witness after another is called, the

Throughout the entire novel, Atticus offers sound advice to his children.

case against Robinson grows. First is Sheriff Heck Tate's testimony. Then Bob Ewell takes the stand, claiming he saw Robinson have sex with his daughter and beat her on the right side of her face. Finally, 19-year-old Mayella Ewell gives her version of what transpired, which is eerily similar to her father's.

Atticus turns the court's attention to Robinson. A tall man who has a mangled left arm because of an

Atticus calmly questions Mayella Ewell in court.

accident with a cotton gin, Robinson shares a different
side of the story. On the night in question, Mayella
invited him in. While the other Ewells were away in
town, he claims she lured him into the house and kissed
him. Then without warning, Bob Ewell burst through
the door, and Robinson ran away.

Atticus presents his closing arguments: Rape can't
be proven because a medical examination hadn't been
done; Robinson couldn't have beaten Mayella with his
crippled left arm; and left-handed Bob Ewell is the real
culprit. As for Mayella, Atticus feels nothing but pity.
When the guilty verdict is read, a disheartened Atticus
pats Robinson on the shoulder and slowly walks out of

the courtroom. Scout turns around from her perch in the colored balcony and is shocked to see that everyone around her is standing in his honor.

Boo Radley Comes Out

Despite Atticus's hope for an appeal, Tom Robinson's fate is sealed. During an exercise period at Enfield Prison Farm, he is shot while trying to escape. A few weeks later, Jem and Scout are accosted in the dark on the way home from a school pageant. Jem is seriously injured. Scout gets away unscathed. Who was the attacker? A deceased Bob Ewell, found with a kitchen knife jammed into his stomach. And who was the mysterious helper responsible for murdering Ewell and saving Scout and Jem? The infamous Boo Radley.

When Atticus hears what happened, he assumes Jem did the stabbing—and he's determined to hold Jem accountable regardless of Ewell's wrongdoing. But Sheriff Tate sets him straight: "There's a black boy dead for no reason, and the man responsible for it's dead," Tate says. "Let the dead bury the dead this time, Mr. Finch."[4] With that, Scout escorts Boo Radley back to his house. Later that night, Atticus reads aloud to Scout as she drifts off to sleep.

5

Atticus Finch: Moral Compass

*M*orality can be defined as a set of principles concerning the distinction between right and wrong or good and bad behavior. When a person has corrupt morals, it means he or she often has dishonest or evil motives and might be prone to acting poorly or even committing crimes. People who have virtuous morals want what's best for themselves and others and will often go out of their way to accomplish good deeds. Throughout history and in many works of art, heroes such as Mother Theresa and Nelson Mandela have been held up as models of humanity precisely because of their moral fortitude—the muscle of their character and their focus on doing what's right.

The character of Atticus Finch, a respected lawyer and defender of blacks, mirrors Lee's own father.

When Nelle Harper Lee wrote *To Kill a Mockingbird*, many readers assumed she based the novel on her childhood. Similar to Scout Finch, Lee grew up in a rural Alabama town in the 1930s, where discrimination ran rampant. Lee's father, Amasa Coleman (A. C.), was similar to Scout's father, Atticus. A. C. was a respected lawyer who faced criticism for defending two black men accused of killing a white shopkeeper.

After *To Kill a Mockingbird* was published in 1960, Harper Lee was praised by critics for taking on the controversial but true-to-life subject of racism in a tight-knit Southern community. The book was also heralded for providing a just and principled message as delivered by its heroic elder protagonist. Atticus Finch is a privileged, educated white lawyer defending a poor, black man's honor. By designating Atticus as the book's hero, Lee lobbies

¿Thesis Statement

The author begins with a short summary of Lee's life as it relates to *To Kill a Mockingbird*. Then at the end of the second paragraph, she states her thesis: "By designating Atticus as the book's hero, Lee lobbies for the inalienable rights of all people regardless of skin color and argues that the most effective way to combat prejudice and bring about positive change is by taking a moral approach." The author will prove that Atticus Finch should be considered a hero because of his sound morals.

for the inalienable rights of all people regardless of skin color and argues that the most effective way to combat prejudice and bring about positive change is by taking a moral approach.

Atticus represents the moral compass in *To Kill a Mockingbird* because he looks beyond narrow-mindedness and acts in accordance with his conscience, even if he must act alone. When Atticus is appointed to defend Tom Robinson's case, rather than conform to the prejudiced opinion in town, he willingly accepts and gives Robinson the best defense possible, despite knowing he will lose. He risks his life to sit outside the jail the night before the trial to protect Robinson from the racist mob. To Atticus, Tom Robinson is guilty of only one thing: being in the wrong place at the wrong time. He is a black man judged and punished because of the color of his skin.

Argument One

Next, the author begins to support her thesis by presenting the first argument: "Atticus represents the moral compass in *To Kill a Mockingbird* because he looks beyond narrow-mindedness and acts in accordance with his conscience, even if he must act alone." The author will show just how brave and admirable Atticus's actions were in the courtroom.

Atticus is willing to put himself in danger to defend Tom Robinson, both in the courtroom and outside of it.

Furthermore, Atticus sets an example in the courtroom by relying on justice and ethics to prove his case. In his closing arguments, he appeals to the jury—and Lee's readers—to consider the right thing to do: "Thomas Jefferson once said that all men are created equal. . . . We know all men are not created equal in the sense some people would have us believe—some people are smarter than others, some people have more opportunity because they're born with it. . . . But there is one way in this country in which all men are created equal. . . . [In] this country our courts are the great levelers, and in our courts all men are created equal."[1]

Atticus is not only a moral man when it serves him in court; his ethics extend to the home as well. At the beginning of the novel, Atticus is revered by Maycomb townsfolk because he is intelligent, fair, and treats each of them—rich or poor—with respect, especially those in the black community. It is for this reason he encourages Scout and Jem to attend Calpurnia's church despite ridicule from Aunt Alexandra and his white neighbors. Atticus feels Calpurnia is a positive influence and an integral member of the Finch family.

Although naturally reserved, Atticus also sets aside time each day for Jem and Scout despite his busy schedule. He teaches them to hold their heads up high and use words instead of fists when dealing with bullies at school. He explains why using derogatory words such as *nigger* is wrong. And he advises against taking

Argument Two

The author then presents the second argument and gives examples of how Atticus acted heroically in other areas of his life: "Atticus is not only a moral man when it serves him in court; his ethics extend to the home as well."

Throughout the novel, Atticus does his best to instill his valuable beliefs in his children.

advantage of those who are less fortunate, less educated, or just plain different, such as Boo Radley.

When Scout questions her father about his reasons for defending Tom Robinson, Atticus's reply is certainly telling: "If I didn't, I couldn't hold up my head in town, I couldn't represent this county in the legislature, I couldn't even tell you or Jem not to do something again."[2] Atticus is the same at home as he is in public, and that's a rare and admirable feat.

Perhaps the most significant example of Atticus's heroism is his understanding that people are inherently flawed and should be praised for their successes and forgiven for their failings. Though some readers might argue he should be less merciful, Atticus doesn't hold a grudge against the prejudiced people of Maycomb who turn their backs on him during the trial. In the case of Mrs. Dubose, Atticus teaches Jem to see Mrs. Dubose's good qualities, not just the bad:

"I wanted you to see what real courage is. . . . It's when you know you're licked before you begin but you begin anyway and you see it through no matter what. . . . Mrs. Dubose won, all ninety-eight pounds of her. . . . she was the bravest person I ever knew."[3]

Atticus also shows compassion for the mob threatening to kill Tom Robinson and the members of the all-white jury who wrongfully convict Robinson for raping Mayella Ewell: "Those are twelve reasonable men in everyday life, Tom's jury, but you saw something come between them and reason. You saw the same thing that night in front of the jail," Atticus explains to Scout and Jem. "There's something in our world that makes men lose their heads—they couldn't be fair if they tried. In our courts, when it's a white man's word against a black man's the white man always wins."[4]

Conclusion

The conclusion reiterates the idea that although Atticus loses the Tom Robinson case, it's because of his strength in morals, focus on helping others, and recognition of both the good and bad in people that make him the book's most heroic character of all—and a model for humanity.

Lee may not agree with all of Atticus's beliefs. She might even argue that he should be more critical, especially toward proven enemies. But by lifting him up as a voice of conscience and reason in a book filled with prejudice—and proving that forgiveness is possible even in the darkest of circumstances—Lee delivers a powerful portrait of one hero's approach to combating evil.

Thinking Critically

Now it's your turn to assess the essay. Consider these questions:

1. The author's thesis statement asserts that Lee argues for the equality of all people regardless of class or skin color and that Atticus should be considered a hero because he's the book's moral compass. Do you think the arguments effectively support this thesis? Why or why not?

2. Over the course of the novel, Atticus forgives many characters. Do you think it's heroic to see the good in all people, even though some might act poorly? Why or why not?

3. The author uses quotes from the book to support her arguments and prove her thesis. Are they successful? Are there others that might be more suitable?

Other Approaches

The previous essay was only one way to analyze the theme of hero as moral compass in *To Kill a Mockingbird*. Another analysis might provide examples of the ways in which Atticus's actions cause others to revise poor behavior and do what's right. Yet another analysis might show how Atticus's insistence on taking the higher road could cause potential problems or bring harm to the people he loves.

Following in a Hero's Footsteps

Heroes usually inspire exemplary behavior in others, even in sticky situations. Despite the embarrassment Scout initially feels for her father because he's old and boring, she proves her growing respect for Atticus by embracing his advice and learning to act in accordance with his moral code. At the beginning of the novel, she solves problems with her fists. By the end, she helps Atticus diffuse the angry mob outside Tom Robinson's jail cell. She also accepts Boo Radley when most others still deem him a monster. Because Scout emulates Atticus and chooses to follow the moral path whenever possible, she can be seen as a hero-in-the-making. A thesis for an essay exploring these ideas might read: By learning from her mistakes and adjusting her behavior to do what's morally correct, Scout is destined to follow in her father's heroic footsteps.

Heroes in Trouble

It's not uncommon for heroes to attract legions of followers. But they can also draw the attention or judgment of sworn enemies. For example, Bob Ewell, who wins the case against Tom Robinson, seeks revenge for being made to look like a fool even after his victory. He spits in Atticus's face, who turns the other cheek. He then goes after Atticus's kids and is killed in the process. Though readers might agree Ewell is an immoral character and deserves his fate, it's important to consider that Atticus may have put Scout and Jem in danger by not recognizing what Ewell was capable of. A possible thesis statement arguing this idea might be: In his actions throughout the book, Atticus proves to readers that sometimes being a hero means taking calculated risks and preparing for disastrous consequences.

6

AN OVERVIEW OF

12 Years a Slave

The 2013 film *12 Years a Slave* is loosely based on a memoir of the same name written by Solomon Northup. Published in 1853, the book tells the story of Northup's misfortune beginning in 1841 when, as a free black man from New York, he was persuaded to travel to Washington, DC, kidnapped, and sold into slavery in rural Louisiana, where he would languish for 12 brutal years.

The film—directed by Steve McQueen and starring Chiwetel Ejiofor as Northup and Lupita Nyong'o as Patsey—won three Academy Awards, including Best Motion Picture of the Year. Though it does take some liberties with presenting the facts of what actually

In the beginning of *12 Years a Slave*, the main character Solomon Northup and his family are free and respected.

happened, the film introduces moviegoers to Solomon Northup's plight and charts his harrowing but steadfast journey to freedom.

Kidnapped

The film begins in Saratoga, New York, in mid-1841. Protagonist Solomon Northup enjoys life as an educated, respected, and prosperous black violinist. One afternoon during a stroll through town, Solomon meets a friend who introduces him to Mr. Brown and Mr. Hamilton, two gentlemen hoping to recruit Solomon to play violin for their traveling circus. Solomon takes the job.

The night before Solomon is set to return home after his trip, the minstrels take him to a fancy Washington, DC, restaurant. "Your generosity is extraordinary," Solomon says to them as they clink glasses.[1] But little does Solomon know they've tricked him and put a sleeping drug in his wine. When he wakes the next morning, he is lying on a cold cellar floor, his feet and hands bound in heavy chains.

"My name is Solomon Northup," he desperately explains to the stranger who soon comes to collect him. "I'm a free man. . . . You have no right whatsoever to detain me." But his cries fall on deaf ears. "You're

Mr. Brown, *left*, and Mr. Hamilton, *right*, trick Solomon, selling him into slavery.

nothin' but a Georgia runaway," the slaver spits out and beats Solomon with such ferocity that the paddle he's using splits in half.[2] The next day, Solomon is forced to board a slave ship bound for Louisiana.

A New Identity

The trip at sea is dreadful. A newfound ally of Solomon's is stabbed to death, and the heat in steerage, where the slaves are kept, is stifling. As soon as the boat docks in Louisiana, Solomon and the other slaves are rounded up, stripped, and prodded by prospective buyers. To disguise his well-to-do roots, Solomon is given the name Platt and sold to plantation owner William Ford. Ford also purchases a woman named Eliza, who sobs when her children are sold off to other buyers.

From the moment Solomon arrives on the plantation and begins work at the timber mill, he refuses to hide his educated status. Against the wishes of John Tibeats, Ford's smarmy lead carpenter, Solomon approaches Ford with an idea to transport cut wood through the bayou. Tibeats is furious and embarrassed to be shown up by a slave. But Ford awards Solomon with a violin in appreciation for his resourcefulness.

Eliza remains inconsolable. When Solomon tries to comfort her and suggests she stop her weeping, they get into an argument. He is rattled further when Eliza insists Ford knows about Solomon's prior life but does nothing to help him.

Solomon refuses to believe Eliza's claims. But his assuredness is tested when he gets into another tangle with Tibeats, who wants to make Solomon pay for his insubordination. When Tibeats accuses Solomon of shoddy carpentry and tries to lash him for it, Solomon grabs the whip out of Tibeats's hand and flogs him. Tibeats retaliates by stringing Solomon up in a tree with a noose around his neck. Before Tibeats can kill him, he is chased away by the plantation overseer, who rescues Solomon but lets him dangle in the scorching sun for hours as punishment for attacking a white man.

After Tibeats criticizes Solomon's work, Solomon defies authority and whips Tibeats.

When Ford returns to the plantation that evening and cuts Solomon down, Solomon begs Ford to help him. Proving Eliza right, Ford refuses and sells Solomon to a neighboring plantation to avoid further controversy.

Another Victim

Solomon misses his family and old life in Saratoga. But with seemingly no hope of being freed, he resigns himself to his situation. He picks cotton in Edwin Epps's fields without complaint and suffers through whippings in silence. Each night, when an intoxicated Epps gathers the slaves together to dance for his amusement, Solomon accompanies the enforced merriment on the violin.

Solomon isn't the only object of Master Epps's attention. Epps is infatuated with a slave named Patsey. When Epps's wife throws a crystal decanter at Patsey's face during a party and orders Epps to sell her, Epps refuses: "Do not set yourself up against Patsey, my dear," he says to his wife. "Because I will rid myself of you well before I do away with her."[3]

Epps's obsession with Patsey grows, and Solomon warns Patsey to steer clear of Epps. But as a slave, she cannot effectively resist. Later that evening, Epps sneaks into the slave quarters and rapes Patsey. After Epps leaves, Patsey tiptoes to Solomon's bedside and begs Solomon to end her life.

Solomon refuses and within weeks, her circumstances grow worse. When she ventures to a neighboring plantation for a bar of soap, a jealous Epps ties her to a post and orders Solomon to beat her. When Solomon's lashes aren't fierce enough, Epps takes over. By the time the punishment is over, Patsey's back is covered in welts.

Escape at Last

For Epps's slaves, the days of picking and hauling cotton grow longer and hotter. Following a stint at a

Even though he sees her in pain, Solomon refuses to take Patsey's life.

neighboring sugar cane plantation, working the fields and getting paid for playing the violin at a high-society party, Solomon returns to Epps's plantation and befriends a white laborer named Armsby who's been hired to pick cotton. Sensing an opportunity, Solomon offers Armsby a deal: if Armsby agrees to send a letter North for Solomon and keeps the deed a secret, Solomon will give him the money he earned at the gala.

Though this attempt to secure his freedom is foiled when Armsby reveals Solomon's intent to Epps, there's another opportunity on the horizon. After Epps hires a white Canadian carpenter named Samuel Bass to construct a gazebo, Solomon tries again to secure an escape. He tells Bass of his situation. Horrified by Solomon's story and agreeing that slavery is evil, Bass agrees to the task.

Just when Solomon starts to think Bass went back on his promise, a horse-drawn carriage clatters up to Epps's plantation with two men from New York inside. Despite Epps's protests, they find out Solomon's true identity and whisk him off to Saratoga. When Solomon is reunited with his family, everyone erupts in tears, surrounding him with love. For Solomon, it seemed like a lifetime since he had been kidnapped. But after 12 impossibly long years, he was home—and finally free.

Before the film's credits roll, a synopsis of what happened after the real Solomon Northup returned home appears on the screen. He brought three men to trial—kidnappers Mr. Brown and Mr. Hamilton, and slave pen owner James Burch. Though he lost the cases, Solomon wasn't deterred. He lectured about the evils of slavery and became an active participant in the Underground Railroad, securing free papers for fugitive slaves. Finally, he hired a white editor named David Wilson to help him publish his memoir in 1853.

Even after 12 years of working as a slave, Solomon never stopped fighting for his freedom.

Northup as Abolitionist Hero

*P*rior to the Civil War (1861–1865) in the United States, hundreds of thousands of black men and women were enslaved against their will by white slave owners. Many were born into slavery. Some spent their lives under the ownership of one master. Others were separated from their families and taken far from their homes. A small portion of the few who managed to escape published firsthand accounts detailing the horrors of their experiences. Including such works as Frederick Douglass's *Narrative of the Life of Frederick Douglass* published in 1845, and *Narrative of William W. Brown, a Fugitive Slave* published in 1847, these oral or written

SOLOMON IN HIS PLANTATION SUIT.

Solomon Northup

The film *12 Years a Slave* is based on Solomon Northup's 1853 memoir.

stories are known as slave narratives. Written for white northerners, they provided a stark contrast to the reports given by Southern plantation owners and were seen as a powerful moral and political argument for the abolition of slavery.

As in the case of most slave narratives, the film *12 Years a Slave*—and the memoir it is based on—is an indictment of racism in the pre-Civil War South. From his abduction through his 12 years spent picking cotton and hacking sugar cane on plantations in Louisiana, Solomon Northup is forced to endure unspeakable suffering because of his race. But unlike other slaves who bear their abuse in silence or become submissive, he fights to gain his freedom so he can share his story with others and help end slavery. It is Solomon's undying belief in racial equality throughout *12 Years a Slave* that paves the way for his salvation, allows

Thesis Statement

The author begins with a short explanation of what a slave narrative is, including the significance of *12 Years a Slave* and its author Solomon Northup in history. Then she states her thesis: "It is Solomon's undying belief in racial equality throughout *12 Years a Slave* that paves the way for his salvation, allows him to instill hope in others, and renders him a hero of the abolitionist movement." The author will prove that Solomon's fight for civil rights despite ill treatment from whites made him stand out as a hero of the antislavery movement.

him to instill hope in others, and renders him a hero of the abolitionist movement.

Throughout his life and despite periods of prolonged torment, Solomon insists on thinking of blacks as equal to whites, even if it means risking his life to speak out against prejudice. At the start of the film, he enjoys luxuries unknown to most blacks, even those residing in the North. He lives in a large house, wears elegant clothing, and doesn't question that he can command the respect of others as an accomplished violinist for high-society parties. But despite his diminished status after he's sold into slavery, Solomon refuses to fully discard his previous identity, risking whippings and even death in favor of preserving his pride.

During the boat voyage from Washington, DC, to Louisiana, a fellow slave shares coping advice with Solomon: "If you want to survive, do and say as little as possible. Tell no one who you really are and tell no one

Argument One

Next, the author supports her thesis by stating the first argument, pointing to the role taking risks and being vocal played in Solomon's heroic push to endure: "Throughout his life and despite periods of prolonged torment, Solomon insists on thinking of blacks as equal to whites, even if it means risking his life to speak out against prejudice."

you can read and write."[1] But instead of heeding the
man's warning and becoming the meek, opinion-less
slave named Platt, Solomon makes calculated moves
to obtain what he knows is rightfully his: freedom.
Unlike Eliza, who crumbles after being separated from
her children, he stays strong: "I survive. I will not fall
into despair. I will offer up my talents to Master Ford.
I will keep myself hearty until freedom is opportune."[2]
He talks back to Tibeats, uses his smarts to offer up
wood-transporting suggestions, and even comes clean
about his privileged roots to Master Ford. "You must
know I am not a slave. Before I came to you, I was a free
man," he says.[3]

Then when he's sold to a different plantation owner
and is faced with worse punishment at the hands of
alcoholic Master Epps, Solomon's determination to
survive still doesn't weaken. He stashes away paper
from his trips into town for Mistress Epps's supplies.
He creates ink out of blackberries. He even asks two
supposedly out-of-reach white men—first Armsby, then
Bass—for help sending a letter North.

Solomon also acts heroically in his dealings with
Patsey by repeatedly trying to convince her she's more
than a piece of property. After being raped by Master

Solomon refuses to accept his fate as a slave, crafting letters in secret to help earn his freedom.

Epps and attacked by Epps's jealous wife during dance parties, Patsey begs Solomon to strangle her. Solomon refuses. Instead he swallows his sympathy and demands that she persevere, restoring a small portion of her dignity despite the hopeless mess she's in.

Patsey's situation grows worse when one day Epps orders Solomon to whip her. Though he does what

Argument Two

The author's second argument reads: "Solomon also acts heroically in his dealings with Patsey by repeatedly trying to convince her she's more than a piece of property." Here, the author discusses how Solomon's actions toward a downtrodden slave inspired her and others to persevere.

he must, Solomon doesn't suffer the shame of whipping her in silence like most other slaves might. He does what Patsey's too afraid to do and screams at Epps: "In the courts of eternal justice, thou shalt answer for this sin!"[4]

Argument Three

The author finishes proving her thesis in her third argument, explaining why continuing to fight for the end of slavery after his rescue indicates Solomon's rare courage: "Finally, despite 12 years in captivity, Solomon doesn't turn vengeful after he is freed; instead he continues to fight against racism, proving the notion that in the rarest of heroes, dignity cannot be squelched by evil."

Finally, despite 12 years in captivity, Solomon doesn't turn vengeful after he is freed; instead he continues to fight against racism, proving the notion that in the rarest of heroes, dignity cannot be squelched by evil. When he reunites with his family, he humbly apologizes for his ragged appearance not because he's ashamed, but because he missed seeing his children grow up and wishes he could've returned sooner.

Solomon's commitment to helping other slaves after he is freed is perhaps the clearest reason he can be called an abolitionist hero. Though it was nearly impossible during that time for a black man to win a case against whites, Solomon took legal action against Mr. Brown

Even though Epps, *left*, forces Solomon to whip Patsey, Solomon refuses to do it in silence.

and Mr. Hamilton because he believed they should be punished for their deception and for their crimes against blacks.

Solomon also took action ushering slaves North through the Underground Railroad. And he hired a white editor to write the introduction for his slave narrative, knowing that it would lend legitimacy to his story. The truth about what happened to Solomon was made available to a wider audience—people who were trying to get slavery abolished.

Conclusion

The conclusion recaps the idea that Solomon deserves the title of abolitionist hero because of his bravery when objecting to blacks' inferiority, willingness to stand up for others, and continued fight to end slavery despite the risks involved.

The movie *12 Years a Slave* is a devastating record of suffering that has happened all too often throughout history. As Solomon Northup says to Samuel Bass, "Slavery is an evil that should befall no one."[5] But it's also a testament to the strength and resilience of the human spirit when fighting for the noble cause of everlasting racial equality. When his slave narrative was published, Solomon became the ultimate hero for the millions of blacks throughout history who stood their ground and fought back against prejudice. He still is to this day.

Thinking Critically

Now it's your turn to assess the essay. Consider these questions:

1. Do you agree with the author's thesis? Can you think of any evidence from the film that could disprove the author's claims?

2. Solomon fought back against his captors many times. He beat Tibeats. He talked back to Master Epps. He sought help from a white abolitionist. Compare his behavior with that of Patsey, who endured her pain in silence. Whose actions do you think are more heroic? Did Patsey have any other recourse?

3. A conclusion should summarize the supporting arguments and partially restate the thesis. Does this conclusion do a good job of summing up the essay? How could it be improved?

Other Approaches

The previous essay was only one example of using a racial and historical lens to analyze the theme of hero in *12 Years a Slave*. Another analysis might examine how Solomon's insistence on remaining independent from his black brethren helps him procure a fate different than theirs. Taking the opposite approach, another analysis might examine the role both blacks and whites played in Solomon's journey to obtain freedom.

Standing Alone

Throughout the film and with the exception of Patsey's company, Solomon mostly sticks to himself. When he works in the fields, he does so alone. During meals, he usually sits by himself or stays quiet. It's only when a fellow slave passes away and Solomon realizes the futility of his situation that he accepts his status and joins the group in singing gospel songs. An argument could be made that it is disengagement and not empathy that allows Solomon to accomplish the most as a hero. A thesis for an essay exploring these ideas might read: Solomon cares deeply about the well-being of fellow blacks, but it's because he stays emotionally and physically detached from other slaves that he is able to escape and become a hero of the abolitionist cause.

Calculated Risks

Despite accomplishing remarkable feats, most heroes don't get where they are in life by acting alone. Some critics might argue that Solomon wouldn't have been able to escape without the help of others, including whites. A possible thesis statement arguing this idea might be: Solomon's heroic behavior hinged on his belief that he would eventually be reunited with his wife and children back home and his willingness to solicit the help of white Canadian laborer Samuel Bass, despite strong potential for failure.

8

AN OVERVIEW OF

The Scarlet Letter and *Little Women*

*N*athaniel Hawthorne's *The Scarlet Letter* (1850) and Louisa May Alcott's *Little Women* (1868) were written during a period in American history known as the New England Renaissance. Hawthorne and Alcott lived in Massachusetts and were transcendentalists, members of a philosophical movement who admired nature and believed thinking and spirituality were more important than materialism and rationalism. Both novels explore these themes and were wildly successful during their time. They are still two of the most widely read works of literature in classrooms across the United States.

In *The Scarlet Letter*, protagonist Hester Prynne is chastised for committing adultery.

The Scarlet Letter: The Punishment

It is June 1642, and the Puritan town of Boston in the Massachusetts Bay Colony is in disarray. A crowd gathers in the square outside the prison. They are waiting for the female convict inside to appear and are gossiping about the punishment that awaits her. One woman suggests she should be branded with an iron. Another calls for something more serious: "This woman has brought shame upon us all and ought to die."[1]

But when Hester Prynne emerges holding her three-month-old baby, Pearl, onlookers gasp at her beauty and dignity. The scarlet *A* embroidered on her dress—a symbol for adultery Hester must wear for the rest of her life—also catches their attention.

With her head held high, Hester steps onto the scaffold in front of the jail and looks out at the crowd. She is shocked to see the grotesque figure of her husband, Roger, who everyone thought was lost at sea and now no longer recognizes. She also spies Reverend Arthur Dimmesdale, the pastor of her congregation as well as Pearl's father. Hester intends to keep his identity secret. "I charge thee to speak out the name of thy fellow-sinner and fellow-sufferer!"[2] Dimmesdale begs her, too weak to expose the truth on his own. But Hester refuses, and when Pearl starts crying, mother and daughter are led back into the jail.

A Seaside Exile

Hester vows to keep the truth about Reverend Dimmesdale hidden. But that doesn't stop her husband from trying to find out who Pearl's father is. Though he accepts the blame for not being a suitable partner for Hester and leaving her alone for too long, he also doesn't want to endure the humiliation of being linked to an adulteress. So he adopts the name Roger Chillingworth to camouflage his identity. When he visits Hester in prison, he informs her of his intent to discover the name of Pearl's father and makes her promise not to interfere.

After her prison term is up, Hester moves to a cottage outside of town. She spends most of her days sewing garments for high-society women. But because of her crime, many of these same women refuse to have anything to do with her socially. They avoid her in town and mock her in church.

Before long, Pearl grows into a pretty but rebellious young girl. When rumors circulate that Pearl should be removed from Hester's care to a more Christian home,

Hester swallows the scorn of her community and focuses on raising her daughter.

Hester journeys to Governor Bellingham's mansion and implores him to reconsider. Pearl pulls a tantrum by answering the catechism incorrectly on purpose. But Reverend Dimmesdale, who is also present, intervenes on Hester's behalf.

Chillingworth Pursues Revenge

As time passes, Reverend Dimmesdale's health declines and Roger Chillingworth, a doctor, moves in with the minister so he can administer constant care. Most townsfolk assume Chillingworth is doing so out of the goodness of his heart. But unbeknownst to Dimmesdale, the conniving doctor suspects the minister of being Pearl's father.

Week after week, Chillingworth probes Dimmesdale's conscience, relentlessly pestering him with questions and hinting at possible wrongdoing. But despite feeling badgered, Dimmesdale never tells Chillingworth the truth. Instead, Chillingworth discovers Dimmesdale's guilt on his own. When he peers beneath the sleeping minister's upper garments during a nap, Chillingworth discovers a scarlet *A* on Dimmesdale's chest.

Dimmesdale's health steadily worsens. Late one night while overcome by shame, he walks to the square where Hester stood to face judgment seven years earlier. As he mounts the scaffold, he sees Hester and Pearl in the moonlight and asks them to join him. Shocked by his broken appearance, Hester silently promises to do what she can to help him—even if it means going to Chillingworth to demand that he call off his quest for revenge.

Days later, Hester meets Dimmesdale in the forest and tells him who Chillingworth really is. Ripping off her scarlet letter, she begs him to run away with her to

Europe so they can start fresh, away from the accusing eyes of their Puritan neighbors. She also officially introduces him to Pearl as the girl's father.

Dimmesdale Confesses

That day in the forest, Dimmesdale agreed to flee with Hester. But after four days of pondering his fate, the minister reconsiders. In the book's climactic final scene, a number of shocking events occur. Dimmesdale delivers a fiery speech on the pulpit. When he's finished, he mounts the scaffold and asks Hester and Pearl to join him. Then he takes off his vestments and reveals his own scarlet A, confesses to his sin and identity as Pearl's father, asks God's forgiveness for Chillingworth, and dies in Hester's arms.

Hawthorne leaves the fate of the other characters up to readers' imaginations. But a careful read suggests the following: consumed by thoughts of revenge, Chillingworth dies and leaves Pearl his money. Pearl travels to Europe with her mother and marries a wealthy man. After years of living abroad, Hester returns to Boston. She lives out the rest of her days in the small cottage, once again with a scarlet *A* embroidered across her chest.

At the end of the novel, Dimmesdale finally comes to terms with his actions, admitting his involvement with Hester.

Little Women: Poor Beginnings

Alcott's two-part novel begins on Christmas Eve as the four March sisters sit by a fire. Sixteen-year-old Meg, the oldest and most motherly of the sisters, works as a nanny to help support the household. Jo, a tomboy and fiercely independent 15-year-old, loves reading books and writing plays for her sisters to perform. Thirteen-year-old Beth is shy and content to play music or help out around the house. The youngest (and vainest) is curly-haired Amy, who dreams of becoming a famous artist. The girls live alone with their mother, whom they call Marmee, while their father serves as a pastor for the Union army on the battlegrounds of the Civil War.

The Marches live a meager existence, particularly when compared to their neighbor, Mr. Laurence, who resides in an extravagant mansion along with his grandson, Theodore, who is known as Laurie. But despite their lack of material comfort, the sisters fill their days with adventures, especially after Jo befriends Laurie at a New Year's Eve party and he joins in on the fun. They create a secret society called the Pickwick Club and publish a makeshift newsletter. In the spring, they go on a picnic with Laurie and his friends.

The March sisters do squabble every now and then—particularly Jo and Amy. One especially awful fight occurs when Amy burns one of Jo's plays after Jo prevents Amy from coming on an outing to a play with Laurie. Later, during an afternoon of ice-skating, Jo retaliates by not telling Amy about a patch of thin ice. When Amy falls through momentarily, Jo is horrified by her own vindictiveness. But try as they may to stay mad

Despite their differences, the March sisters and their mother are very close.

The March sisters' strong bond helps them get through many tough times throughout the novel, including Amy's fall through the ice.

at each other, one sister always gives in, and Marmee does her best to make sure her children feel loved.

Mixed Blessings

In November, the Marches' lives take a turn for the worse. Marmee receives a telegram from the front, revealing Mr. March has fallen ill. Because Jo knows her mother doesn't have enough money, she cuts her hair and sells it to help pay for the trip to see Mr. March. Accompanied by Laurie's tutor, Mr. John Brooke, Marmee journeys to the hospital in Washington, DC, to take care of her husband.

While Marmee is away, another tragedy befalls the family. Beth comes down with scarlet fever after babysitting a neighbor's sick infant. Meg and Jo do what they can to look after their sister, but Amy is sent to live with Aunt March until Beth's health returns. Though her fever finally breaks, Beth's strength and vigor never fully recover, and Marmee, who rushes back to be by her side, vows to keep vigilant watch over her frail daughter.

As the year comes to a close and Christmas arrives, the March family once again counts their blessings. With Mr. March home for a respite, the girls luxuriate in spending time with their father. Beth feels well enough to play the piano. After John Brooke expresses an interest in asking for her hand in marriage, Meg contemplates the idea of becoming a mature woman. And Jo tries extra hard not to feel saddened by the idea of losing her sister to a man.

Big Changes

The second half of *Little Women* unfolds three years later, and all the March girls, rejoined by their father, are in for big changes—and a number of challenges. For one, Meg officially becomes Mrs. Brooke. With marriage comes more responsibilities—a new home, a husband with different needs, piles of bills, and children—twins nicknamed Daisy and Demi.

But Meg isn't the only one with marriage on the mind. After years of masking his true feelings, Laurie reveals his love for Jo. Rather than fall prey to romance, however, Jo rejects her longtime friend. Instead she heads to New York for the winter, works as a governess, and starts writing sensationalist stories for a local publication. When she returns home months later and informs Laurie she's still not the marrying type, he sails off to Europe to pursue his passion for music and mend his broken heart.

Then tragedy strikes. Beth, who has never fully recovered from her bout with scarlet fever, grows increasingly ill and dies. Amy, who has been traveling in Europe with the girls' Aunt Carroll, rushes to return home but is persuaded by Marmee to stay overseas. During her travels, she reunites with Laurie and strikes up a deeper friendship, which soon turns into love. A year later, the two marry and return home.

Life Goes On

At the end of the novel, the March girls' lives aren't what they'd expected. But each sister is satisfied with

Instead of agreeing to marry, Jo moves to New York to work and write, following a different path than her sisters.

her lot. Meg and John have worked out the kinks in their marriage. Laurie and Amy are in love and have a daughter. Even Jo finds fulfillment. She marries Professor Bhaer, her German tutor in New York, has two children, and opens a school for boys. In the last scene, Mrs. March celebrates her sixtieth birthday around the table, enjoying her time with her family.

9

Feminist Icons

$\mathcal{T}$hroughout history, women have often been viewed as subservient to men. To put it in simplistic terms, men did the work while women stayed at home. But can women find happiness without getting married or be taken seriously pursuing a career? Feminists say yes. When analyzing literature through a feminist lens, it is often the characters who intentionally avoid preferred social norms—or stretch the boundaries of gender stereotypes—who turn out to be the most heroic.

During the mid- and late-1800s, when authors Nathaniel Hawthorne and Louisa May Alcott were writing their novels, most women were expected to adhere to set rules in order to live a full life: observe social etiquette, marry young, and act the faithful subordinate wife and mother to your family. Let the man do the rest. But when *The Scarlet Letter* and *Little Women*

Jo March rejects society's expectations of her, even dressing more masculine than other women of her time.

Thesis Statement

At the end of the first paragraph, the author states her thesis: "Because Hester Prynne and Jo March ignore society's expectations and stand by their own choices regarding love and work, they can be considered feminist icons of their time." The author will prove Hester and Jo are feminist heroes because of their fearless courage to be different.

Argument One

Next, the author begins to support her thesis by presenting the first argument: "Hester and Jo epitomize the feminist hero by going against established gender stereotypes in order to advance their own agendas." She supports the thesis by providing examples of Hester and Jo's willingness to bend the rules of what it means to be female.

were published, readers were surprised to find two female protagonists who did nothing of the sort. Instead, these women are empowered and independent. Because Hester Prynne and Jo March ignore society's expectations and stand by their own choices regarding love and work, they can be considered feminist icons of their time.

Hester and Jo epitomize the feminist hero by going against established gender stereotypes in order to advance their own agendas. By choosing to have sex outside her unhappy marriage and wearing the scarlet *A* despite constant ridicule from her Puritan neighbors, Hester proves she's willing to take her life

Throughout *The Scarlet Letter,* Hester's character proves time and time again that she is capable of raising her daughter alone.

and femininity into her own hands. When she refuses to reveal the name of her secret lover and share the blame, it is a testament to her strength of character that she faces her demons head-on and shoulders the full weight of her actions. Finally, her determination to raise Pearl on her own sends a powerful feminist message: she is capable of raising her child without the normally required help of a man.

While Jo's rebellion isn't as drastic, she too ignores what society expects of her if it doesn't serve her purpose. Unlike Meg or Amy, who adore flouncing around in fancy clothes to attract male attention, Jo wears a burned dress to a New Year's Eve party. She hates needlework and housework, as Beth is content to do. And while most girls her age, such as Meg or Amy, would be delighted to have a male suitor propose marriage, Jo repeatedly pushes away Laurie because she doesn't share his feelings.

Argument Two

The author then presents the second argument by explaining how having a passion for work made Hester and Jo stand out: "Both Hester and Jo further prove their feminist leanings by choosing to work despite others' disapproval."

Both Hester and Jo further prove their feminist leanings by choosing to work despite others' disapproval. Rather than suffer her punishment in shame, Hester willfully rebels by embroidering a scarlet *A* on her chest, accented by a radiant gold thread. She uses her talents as a seamstress and makes a living sewing baby clothes and dresses for the women in town. Ironically, the same women who judge Hester for being an adulteress support Hester and her illegitimate child by making use of her services and buying her dresses.

So, too, Jo defies the patriarchal society in which she was raised by pursuing work over what society calls more acceptable pastimes. She spends her childhood writing plays in the attic instead of going to balls or courting men. During a time when most women didn't dare travel on their own, Jo winters in New York, writing sensationalist pop stories and getting published. And unlike Meg, who settles into the role of dutiful wife, Jo bravely contemplates a career as a professional writer.

It's Hester and Jo's concerted efforts to adapt and evolve as they grow older—embracing some rules and discarding others—that render them true feminist heroes. After Dimmesdale dies, Hester decides to make the journey and flee to Europe with her daughter as planned even without Dimmesdale.

Argument Three

The author finishes proving her thesis by providing a third argument, mainly that Hester and Jo's ability to change over time are what make them heroic: "It's Hester and Jo's concerted efforts to adapt and evolve as they grow older—embracing some rules and discarding others—that render them true feminist heroes."

In a way, Jo gives up her dream of becoming a famous writer in favor of getting married. But rather than blindly agreeing to wed any suitor, Jo learns to grasp marriage's benefits and chooses a husband on her own terms. It's precisely because she realizes she wants some form of what her sisters Meg and Amy have—and understands that it doesn't have to end in her own domestication or subordination—that Jo is able to evolve into a stronger, more mature woman.

Hester Prynne and Jo March aren't flawless feminist characters. In fact, some critics might argue that both women conform in the end. But each embarks on a journey to define her self-worth. By perpetually questioning society's expectations and having the courage to stand on their own in matters of work and love, Hester and Jo can be considered heroes.

Conclusion

The conclusion reiterates the idea that Hester Prynne and Jo March epitomize the feminist ideal by having the courage to march to the beat of their own drums despite rigid definitions of how a woman should act.

Thinking Critically

Now it's your turn to assess the essay. Consider these questions:

1. The author's thesis statement claims Hester Prynne and Jo March are examples of feminist icons. Do you think this is a valid thesis? Why or why not?

2. What is the author's strongest argument? Which is the weakest? What other evidence from the texts could be used to support the thesis?

3. In the final argument, the author suggests Hester and Jo's willingness to embrace some of society's rules renders them true feminist heroes. Is this a successful tactic or does it disprove the thesis?

Other Approaches

The previous essay was only one way to analyze the theme of feminist hero in *The Scarlet Letter* and *Little Women*. Another analysis might compare the ways in which Hester and Jo use their contrasting strengths to get ahead. Another analysis might explore more deeply how Hester and Jo's actions toward the end of each novel affect their standing as feminist icons.

Body vs. Mind

It can be assumed that Hester Prynne is a sexual woman. After all, despite her chastity throughout *The Scarlet Letter*, it is her choice to give in to her lust that enables her to become a mother. In contrast, Jo March is more concerned with matters of the head. For most of *Little Women*, she shuns a physical relationship with Laurie in favor of pursuing her writing. Yet both Hester and Jo find fulfillment in the end. A thesis for an essay exploring these ideas might read: Hester and Jo are both strong and heroic women, though it can be argued Hester's drive is physical while Jo's is psychological.

Embracing Faults

Most people who are shunned by their community might opt to start over by adopting a new, untarnished life elsewhere with less judgment. But what happens when characters face their shortcomings head on? Maybe owning up to faults paves the way for greater happiness in the end. For example, Hester is unable to survive on her own after Pearl is married, and Jo recognizes her loneliness once her sisters are married off. A possible thesis statement arguing this idea might be: Hester and Jo can be admired for their self-reliance, but it is their social dependence on others that highlights a more human side of the feminist hero.

Analyze It!

Now that you have examined the theme of the hero, are you ready to perform your own analysis? You have read that this type of evaluation can help you look at literature in a new way and make you pay attention to certain issues you may not have otherwise recognized. So, why not look for a hero theme in one or more of your favorite books?

First, choose the work you want to analyze. Who is the main hero? Are there secondary heroes? Do characters grow or change through inner or moral quests? If you choose to compare the theme in more than one work, what do they have in common? How do they differ? Next, write a specific question about the theme that interests you. Then you can form your thesis, which should provide the answer to that question. Your thesis is the most important part of your analysis and offers an argument about the work, considering the theme, its effect on the characters, or what it says about society or the world. Recall that the thesis statement typically appears at the very end of the introductory paragraph of your essay. It is usually only one sentence long.

After you have written your thesis, find evidence to back it up. Good places to start are in the work itself or in journals or articles that discuss what other people have said about it. You may also want to read about the author or creator's life so you can get a sense of what factors may have affected the creative process. This can be especially useful if you are considering how the theme connects to history or the author's intent.

You should also explore parts of the book that seem to disprove your thesis and create an argument against them. As you do this, you might want to address what others have written about the book. Their quotes may help support your claim.

Before you start analyzing a work, think about the different arguments made in this book. Reflect on how evidence supporting the thesis was presented. Did you find that some of the techniques used to back up the arguments were more convincing than others? Try these methods as you prove your thesis in your own critique.

When you are finished writing your critique, read it over carefully. Is your thesis statement understandable? Do the supporting arguments flow logically, with the topic of each paragraph clearly stated? Can you add any information that would present your readers with a stronger argument in favor of your thesis? Were you able to use quotes from the book, as well as from other critics, to enhance your ideas? Did you see the work in a new light?

Glossary

abolitionist
Someone who works to put an end to slavery.

adultery
Sex between a married person and someone who is not that person's wife or husband.

catechism
A collection of questions and answers that are used to teach people about the Christian religion.

derogatory
Expressing a low opinion of someone or something; showing a lack of respect for someone or something.

discrimination
The practice of unfairly treating a person or group of people differently from other people or groups of people.

epitome
A perfect example; an example that represents or expresses something very well.

ethics
Rules of behavior based on ideas about what is morally good and bad.

feminism
The belief that men and women should have equal rights and opportunities.

humility
The quality or state of not thinking you are better than other people; a state of being humble.

inalienable
Impossible to take away or give up.

insubordination
The act of not obeying authority or refusing to follow orders.

lynch
To kill someone illegally as punishment for a crime.

morality
Beliefs about what is right behavior and what is wrong behavior.

precocious
Showing the qualities and abilities of an adult at a young age.

prejudice
An unfair feeling of dislike for a person or group because of race, sex, or religion.

racism
Poor treatment of or violence against people because of their race.

stereotype
An often unfair and untrue belief that many people have about all people or things with a particular characteristic—for example, gender or race.

subservient
Very willing or too willing to obey someone else; less important than something or someone else.

Underground Railroad
A system of cooperation among active abolitionists in the United States before 1863 by which fugitive slaves were secretly helped to reach the North or Canada.

Characteristics
AND CLASSICS

The hero is a common theme in literature. Heroic characters in literature, art, and film are those who accomplish extraordinary deeds. Authors and film directors use heroic characters to provide examples of model behavior.

This theme often includes:

- A main character, who serves as the work's hero
- A call to action or journey the hero must embark upon
- Antagonists, or enemies, the hero must confront
- Challenges or obstacles the hero must overcome

Some famous works with a hero theme are:

- Homer's *The Odyssey*
- Mark Twain's *The Adventures of Huckleberry Finn*
- J. R. R. Tolkien's The Lord of the Rings series
- Suzanne Collins's The Hunger Games trilogy
- *The Avengers*
- *Guardians of the Galaxy*

References

Alcott, Louisa May. *Little Women*. New York: Grosset & Dunlap, 1947. Print.

Campbell, Joseph. *The Hero with a Thousand Faces*. Princeton, NJ: Princeton UP, 1972. Print.

Harry Potter and the Sorcerer's Stone. Dir. Chris Columbus. Perf. Daniel Radcliffe, Rupert Grint, Emma Watson, Richard Harris, and Maggie Smith. Warner Bros, 2001. DVD.

Hawthorne, Nathaniel. *The Scarlet Letter*. New York: Penguin Books, 2003. Print.

Lee, Harper. *To Kill a Mockingbird: 50th Anniversary Edition*. New York: HarperCollins, 2010. Print.

12 Years a Slave. Dir. Steve McQueen. Perf. Chiwetel Ejiofor, Lupita Nyong'o, Michael Kenneth Williams, and Michael Fassbender. Twentieth Century Fox, 2013. DVD.

Additional
RESOURCES

Further Readings

Hey, Boo: Harper Lee and 'To Kill a Mockingbird.' Dir. Mary McDonagh Murphy. Perf. Mary Badham, Rick Bragg, Alice Lee, Tom Brokaw, Oprah Winfrey. First Run Features, 2011. DVD.

Northup, Solomon. *Twelve Years a Slave*. New York: Penguin, 2012. Print.

Peterson-Hilleque, Victoria. *Essential Critiques: How to Analyze the Works of J. K. Rowling.* Minneapolis, MN: Abdo, 2012. Print.

Rowling, J. K. *Harry Potter and the Sorcerer's Stone*. New York: Scholastic, 1997. Print.

Websites

To learn more about Essential Literary Themes, visit **booklinks.abdopublishing.com**. These links are routinely monitored and updated to provide the most current information available.

Places to Visit

Louisa May Alcott's Orchard House
399 Lexington Road
Concord, MA 01742
978-369-4118
http://www.louisamayalcott.org
Walk through the rooms where the Alcott family ate and slept
from 1858 to 1877.

National Civil Rights Museum at the Lorraine Motel
450 Mulberry Street
Memphis, TN 38103
901-521-9699
http://civilrightsmuseum.org
This premiere institution walks visitors through decades of civil
rights history, from the origins of slavery through the Civil War,
the civil rights movement, and into the race problems of today.

The Wizarding World of Harry Potter
Universal Studios Theme Park
6000 Universal Boulevard
Orlando, FL 32819
407-363-8000
https://www.universalorlando.com/Theme-Parks/Wizarding-
World-Of-Harry-Potter.aspx
Find replicas of platform 9¾, Diagon Alley, the Hogwarts Express,
and Hogwarts!

Source Notes

Chapter 1. Introduction to Themes in Literature

None.

Chapter 2. An Overview of *Harry Potter and the Sorcerer's Stone*

1. J. K. Rowling. "Timeline: Harry Potter and the Sorcerer's Stone." *JKRowling.com.* J. K. Rowling Website Limited, 2012. Web. 14 Jan. 2015.

2. *Harry Potter and the Sorcerer's Stone*. Dir. Chris Columbus. Perf. Daniel Radcliffe, Rupert Grint, Emma Watson, Richard Harris, and Maggie Smith. Warner Bros., 2001. DVD.

3. Ibid.

4. Ibid.

Chapter 3. Harry Potter as Anti-Archetype

1. *Harry Potter and the Sorcerer's Stone*. Dir. Chris Columbus. Perf. Daniel Radcliffe, Rupert Grint, Emma Watson, Richard Harris, and Maggie Smith. Warner Bros., 2001. DVD.

Chapter 4. An Overview of *To Kill a Mockingbird*

1. Harper Lee. *To Kill a Mockingbird: 50th Anniversary Edition*. New York: HarperCollins, 2010. Print. 6.

2. Ibid. 117.

3. Ibid. 120.

4. Ibid. 317.

Chapter 5. Atticus Finch: Moral Compass

1. Harper Lee. *To Kill a Mockingbird: 50th Anniversary Edition*. New York: HarperCollins, 2010. Print. 233.

2. Ibid. 87.

3. Ibid. 128.

4. Ibid. 250.

Chapter 6. An Overview of *12 Years a Slave*

1. *12 Years a Slave*. Dir. Steve McQueen. Perf. Chiwetel Ejiofor, Lupita Nyong'o, Michael Kenneth Williams, and Michael Fassbender. Twentieth Century Fox, 2013. DVD.
2. Ibid.
3. Ibid.

Chapter 7. Northup as Abolitionist Hero

1. *12 Years a Slave*. Dir. Steve McQueen. Perf. Chiwetel Ejiofor, Lupita Nyong'o, Michael Kenneth Williams, and Michael Fassbender. Twentieth Century Fox, 2013. DVD.
2. Ibid.
3. Ibid.
4. Ibid.
5. Ibid.

Chapter 8. An Overview of *The Scarlet Letter* and *Little Women*

1. Nathanial Hawthorne. *The Scarlet Letter*. New York: Penguin, 2003. Print. 49.
2. Ibid. 62.

Chapter 9. Feminist Icons

None.

Index

About the Author

Alexis Burling has written dozens of articles and books for young readers on a variety of topics ranging from current events and famous people, to nutrition and fitness, careers and money management, relationships, and cooking. When Burling was in school, her favorite subject was English. She loved reading, analyzing books and movies, and writing papers just like you see in this book. In fact, she enjoyed the activity so much she became a professional book critic! Her reviews of both adult and young adult books, author interviews, and other publishing industry-related articles have been published in the *New York Times*, *Washington Post*, and *Chicago Tribune*.